A288

D1368902

Cover illustration: During the late 1970s, a sergeant of the 7th
Special Forces Group prepares to destroy a target after placing
charges on it. Note the red beret flash of the 7th SFG and the Uzi
SMG. (US Army)

1. A Navy SEAL is inserted for a mission by rapelling from a helicopter, January 1967. (US Navy)

UNIFORMS ILLUSTRATED NO. 3

US
SPECIAL FORCES
1945 to the present

LEROY THOMPSON

ARMS AND ARMOUR PRESS

Introduction

Uniforms Illustrated 3: US Special Forces, 1945 to the present
Published by Arms and Armour Press Limited,
Link House, West Street, Poole, Dorset
BH15 1LL.

Distributed in the USA by Sterling Publishing Co.
Inc., 2 Park Avenue, New York, NY 10016.

Distributed in Australia by Capricorn Link
(Australia) Pty. Ltd., P.O. Box 665, Lane Cove,
New South Wales 2066, Australia.

First published 1984. Reprinted 1987.

British Library Cataloguing in Publication Data:
Thompson, Leroy
U.S. Special Forces, 1945 to the Present –
(Uniforms illustrated; 3)
1. United States. *Army. Special Forces* – History
I. Title   II. Series
356′.167′0973   U262

ISBN 0-85368-625-4

Edited by Michael Boxall; designed by Roger
Chesneau; printed and bound in Great Britain by
William Clowes Limited, Beccles.

Although American élite troops, such as Rogers' Rangers, date back to the French and Indian Wars, modern US élite forces trace their lineage to the paratroops, Rangers, OSS, and 1st Special Service Force of the Second World War. Since the end of that war, US airborne and élite forces have both seen combat and served as 'advisers'.

Each of the four US branches of service has its own integral airborne and élite forces. The Army has the largest contingent in the 82nd Airborne Division and the 101st Airborne Division (Airmobile). In addition there are smaller independent parachute units and the 75th Rangers, the Special Forces, and divisional Recondos. The US Marines consider the entire Corps an élite fighting force, but the *crème de la crème* of the Marines are the Recons and Force Recons who are trained for beach reconnaissance and other long-range patrol or raiding missions. The Navy's SEALs (Sea, Air, Land), though small in numbers, are among the most highly trained élite forces in the world. Navy UDT (Underwater Demolition Team) units are also highly skilled and trained. The US Air Force's élite formations are less well-known than those of the other branches, but are still highly deserving of their élite status. Air Force Parachute Jumpers – more formally known as Pararescuemen – rescue downed aircrew under any conditions, even under fire. In addition to being trained as parachutists, combat swimmers, mountain troops, ski troops, etc., the PJs are also trained in emergency medical techniques. Air Force CCTs (Combat Control Team members) are also trained as paratroopers, combat swimmers, and Rangers, but in addition receive training which enables them to call in airstrikes even deep in enemy-controlled territory. Air Force Combat Weather Teams are even less widely known though trained along lines similar to the CCTs. One final Air Force unit which should be mentioned is the Combat Security Police. Disbanded after the Vietnam War, CSPs were an élite Ranger-trained light infantry strike unit, highly skilled in ambush and patrol.

Because of the dangerous and special nature of the missions assigned to airborne and élite forces and the necessity for teamwork combined with individual initiative, distinctive uniforms and insignia have often been used to foster ésprit de corps. Berets, for example, are worn by many of the US élite formations: green, Special Forces; black, Rangers; maroon, 82nd Airborne and Air Force PJs and CCTs; dark blue, formerly Air Force CCTs and CSPs; and grey, Air Force Combat Weather. The 101st Airborne (Airmobile) has also worn a blue beret.

Even before camouflage utilities were the norm, élite and airborne units could often be identified by the use of 'cammies', especially 'tiger stripes' or 'duck hunter' patterns during the Vietnam War. Colourful distinctive insignia, and, of course, parachutist's wings as well as highly-polished jump boots with trousers bloused into them have often been the sign of the élite fighting man, whilst the distinctive dagger or fighting knife still holds a special symbolism in some élite formations.

Leroy Thompson, 1984

2. A member of the 173rd Airborne Brigade silhouetted against the setting sun as he stands guard duty in Vietnam. (US Army)

▲3 ▼4

3. In March 1951, men of the 187th Airborne Regimental Combat Team prepare to make a practice jump on the airstrip at Taegu, Korea. The 187th RCT, formerly part of the 11th Airborne Division, made the only large-scale combat jumps of the Korean War. These men are still wearing the Second World War T7 parachute harness. Note also that only a small rucksack is slung below the reserve parachute. The second man from the left is probably a medic rather than a chaplain as the cross on his helmet might indicate. (US Army)

4. Men of the 1st Airborne Ranger Company check their parachutes prior to a jump at Yoju, Korea, in April 1951. Some Airborne Rangers jumped with the 187th RCT on its drops at Sukchon and Musan-Ni. (US Army)

5. Men of the 3rd Ranger Company, 3rd Infantry Division

prepare for a patrol across the Imjin River, April 1951. During the Korean War US airborne forces switched from their Second World War tan utilities to the standard green, which provided better camouflage. In this photograph the sergeant in the middle foreground wears airborne and Ranger tabs over his 3rd Division shoulder-sleeve insignia. The man in the left foreground is armed with a Browning Automatic Rifle. (US Army)

6. Men of the 1st Airborne Ranger Company pick up parachutes prior to a practice jump in Korea, April 1951. They are wearing standard green utilities and green fatigue hat. Although the hat is sometimes associated with the Rangers, it was certainly not distinctive to them. The weapons shown here are M1 Garand rifles. (US Army)

▲7

7. Men of the 187th RCT wait in a C-119 for take-off prior to making a jump, March 1951. The soldier in the middle on the right wears one of the caps with earflaps familiar to viewers of the television series 'MASH'. (US Army)

8. Members of the 2nd Ranger Company man a .30 calibre light machine-gun in central Korea, February 1951. The Korean War was the first integrated war fought by the US Army. Ranger companies were among the easiest to integrate because each man had to meet tough requirements to qualify. Historically there has been less racial tension in élite units than in others, which is attributable to the fact that a man must earn the right to serve in one. The 173rd Airborne Brigade in Vietnam, for example, prided itself on its bi-racial make-up. (US Army)

9. Another view of the 187th RCT preparing for a jump helps convey the ruggedness of the terrain in Korea, March 1951. (US Army)

10. Men of the 3rd Ranger Company scout Chinese positions and radio information to artillery units. The man on the left is armed with the M1D sniper's version of the Garand rifle. Note the utility caps, which were to some extent identified with the Rangers. (US Army)

▼8

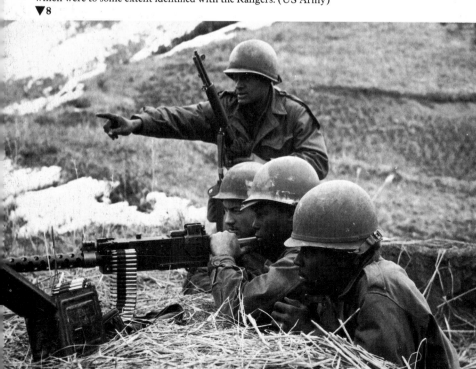

▲11 ▼12

11. This photograph, which dates from the early 1950s, is one of the earliest showing Special Forces wearing berets. Their camouflage is the commercially available 'duck hunter' pattern. The beret is green. Note that US basic airborne wings are here worn as a beret badge. Members of the Special Forces are often equipped with diverse weapons. Here for example, the man at the right carries an M1 Carbine, while the man on the left has what appears to be a Czech Model 23 9mm SMG. Note that .45 automatics are also carried. (Society of Vietnamese Rangers)

12. A USMC Recon patrol moves through elephant grass while patrolling in Vietnam near the Demilitarized Zone and the border with Laos. As is evident from this photograph, the long-range patrol missions undertaken by Marine Recons, often demanded that they hump a heavy load of equipment. These men are wearing standard USMC fatigues, but with the boonie hat rather than a steel helmet or fatigue cap. The Marine bringing up the rear carries the radio; note the telephone cord passing beneath his right arm. (USMC)

13. The insignia for MACV SOG (Military Assistance Command Vietnam Special Operations Group), used in the mid to late 1960s, though to cloud the unit's function it was also known as Studies and Observation Group. The Master pilot's wings represent the involvement of the Air Force, the fouled anchor that of the Navy and Marine Corps, and the death's head wearing a green beret on the shell burst, that of Special Forces. As with all SOG insignia, this one was usually worn sewn to the lining of the beret, inside a utility jacket, or on a 'party suit'.

14. This NVA/VC rucksack (c1960s) was very similar to some manufactured in Korea for use by Special Forces personnel and the local indigenous personnel they trained. Such rucks had two advantages: first, they were designed for the smaller Asian personnel and hence would not be too heavy; and second, their profile would not betray a member of Special Forces or Vietnamese striker if spotted in the jungle by an NVA or VC patrol. Such indigenous rucksacks were especially popular with Roadrunner units which dressed in VC-style clothing and operated along VC trail networks. (West Point Museum)

15. Standing on the 'slick's' runners, air cavalrymen of the 1st Air Cavalry prepare for a fast dismount as they assault into a 'hot' LZ west of Duc Pho, Quang Ngai Province, Republic of Vietnam. Note the 'bug juice' bottle tucked into the rubber band around the helmet of the first man on the Huey's left runner. (US Army)

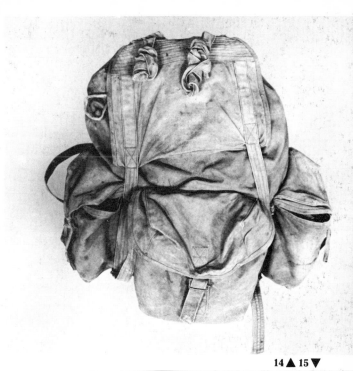

13 ▲

14 ▲ 15 ▼

◄16

17▲

16. A US Navy SEAL trainee practises patrol tactics in California. He wears the four-colour leaf-pattern camouflage which became available to élite forces during 1968. (US Navy)
17. A US Navy SEAL brings in a Viet Cong suspect, September 1967. SEALs wore diverse headgear, but this one has chosen an OD boonie hat. He carries an M16 which, although the standard rifle in Vietnam, was not necessarily the choice of most SEALs. He also appears to be wearing the USMC flak jacket. (US Navy)

▲18 ▼19

18. The insignia worn by members of Recon Team Fork during the Vietnam War. The shell burst – in this case yellow – with the death's head wearing a green beret was a common motif on RT insignia. Such patches were not normally worn openly, especially on operations. Frequently, however, the insignia was sewn inside the beret.

19. Insignia of Recon Team Missouri, Vietnam era. One oddity about this insignia is that CCN Recon teams were usually named after types of snake (note the snake curling around the skull on this insignia), while CCC teams were named after American states.

20. An unauthorized shoulder-sleeve insignia worn by 173rd Airborne Brigade snipers in Vietnam during the 1960s. Note that a scoped rifle has replaced the sword usually gripped by the wing, and the word 'sniper' has been added.

21. Insignia of Recon Team Weather, which was assigned to Command and Control South, at Ban Me Thuot. CCS Recon teams had names such as RT Spike, RT Weather, RT Plane, RT Lightning, and so on.

22. Although the USMC historically wears far fewer insignia than the other branches of the armed forces, in Vietnam the Recons did have a few distinctive patches, such as this one belonging to the 2nd Recon Battalion.

23. At the top is the original Trojan Horse beret badge worn by the 10th Special Forces Group during the 1950s, before the advent of flashes. The Trojan Horse represented the Special Forces's mission of training guerillas to strike from within an occupied country. At the left is a later version of the Trojan Horse beret badge, worn with a flash. At the right is the beret badge of the Special Warfare Center (also known as the John F. Kennedy Center for Military Assistance, and lately redesignated 1st Special Operations Command (SOCOM) (Airborne) (Provisional)). This badge is still worn.

20▲ 21▼

22▲ 23▼

▲24 ▼25

24. A river patrol unit trained and advised by US Special Forces, July 1967. The spotted camouflage worn by these members of a MIKE Force was most commonly seen on members of the PRUs (Provincial Recon Units) or the National Police Field Force. The MIKE Force insignia worn on the beret of the man in the right foreground was often worn on the pocket by US Special Forces advisers. Camouflage berets such as these men wear were also worn by US Navy SEALs, US Army LRRPs, and US Army Special Forces. (US Army)

25. April 1969. While in training, two members of the 82nd Airborne Division fire the .45 automatic pistol. Note the highly-polished jump boots, which were a trademark of the airborne divisions, and the bloused trousers of the paratroopers. The 82nd Airborne insignia is visible on the left shoulder of the instructor (right). (US Army)

26. During 'Operation Oregon', April 1967, members of the 1st Airborne Cavalry hit an LZ as part of a search-and-destroy mission in Quang Ngai Province, Republic of Vietnam. The air cavalryman in the foreground is armed with an M16 with the M203 40mm grenade-launcher mounted. The ammunition slung round his torso is for the M60 GPMG. (US Army)

▲27

▲28 ▼29

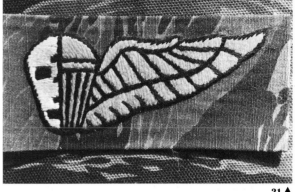

30▲

31▲

27. Standard and subdued Vietnam era shoulder insignia of those who had completed special jungle survival and operations training. Normally, this training was given in Panama, but during the Vietnam War some jungle training was also conducted at Clark AFB in the Philippines and at the MACV Recondo School at Nha Trang. Normally, however, the 'JUNGLE EXPERT' insignia indicated a graduate of the school in Panama.

28. At left is the US Navy SEAL breast badge, worn in gold by officers, and silver by enlisted personnel. The trident and anchor represent sea capability; the eagle, air capability; and the pistol, land capability. At the right is the badge worn by the UDTs, also in gold or silver.

29. 1968. A trooper of the 173rd Airborne Brigade during the fight for Hill 882 in Vietnam. Note that for close-quarters work he carries a Stevens 12 gauge fighting shotgun. Note also the angle-headed flashlight worn on his webbed gear. The M16 round in the rubber band of his helmet was less typical than the wearing of a a bottle of insect repellent. (US Army)

30. On the left are US parachutist's basic wings which have had a gold wash applied and a tiny USMC emblem affixed. These non-standard wings were worn by some Marine parachute units. At the right are the current official US Navy/USMC parachutist's wings.

31. Cloth wings worn by USMC Recons in Vietnam. These wings are sometimes found on various camouflage patterns, in this case tiger stripes.

32. Two trainees at the MACV/Recondo School at Nha Trang await exfiltration after a three-day 'final exams' on the island of Hon Tre, December 1969. The leaf-pattern camouflage utilities probably indicate that these men will be assigned to either a LRRP or Ranger company. Note the much-worn boonie hat on the man at the right. (US Army)

32▼

▲33

33. US Navy SEALs, dressed in tiger stripe camouflage utilities, adjust their gas masks as they rehearse for a search-and-destroy operation. The gas masks indicate the possibility of going into VC tunnel complexes (US Navy)

34. USMC Recons cross a river ahead of a larger Marine force in 1965. Note that unlike Recons on a deep penetration mission, these Recons are lightly equipped for scouting. Standard green fatigues and fatigue hats are worn. The Recon in the left foreground appears to have a mini-smoke grenade taped to his

combat braces. The craft is an IBS (Inflatable Boat, Small) of the type used by the USMC.

35. A pair of US Marine Recons on an Intelligence-gathering operation in the mid 1950s, offer one very interesting innovation. To provide camouflage headgear they have converted standard USMC helmet covers to caps. The man on the right is armed with the M3 .45 calibre SMG, often known as the 'grease gun'. (USMC)

▼ 34   35 ▶

▲36 ▼37   ▼38

36. A USMC Recon of the Vietnam era observes enemy positions and maps them using different coloured pencils. Although Recons are formidable fighters they are primarily trained for infiltration to gather intelligence or to call in air strikes, naval or artillery fire. (USMC)

37. A Special Forces sergeant, first class instructs members of Mobile Strike Force (MIKE Force) members in hand-to-hand combat, December 1967. Green beret and green utilities are worn. Note that on his right shoulder this sergeant wears the 3rd Infantry Division insignia indicating that he has seen combat with that unit, probably in Korea. (US Army)

38. On the left is the standard Special Forces beret badge still worn today; on the right is a beret flash of the 5th SFG, locally made in South-east Asia, with the beret badge sewn in.

39. During the late 1960s, indigenous troops of a SOG recon team with their US Special Forces leader, on the right. OD head scarves instead of other headgear are worn by most of the team. Note also the STABO rigs which were designed so that helicopter extractions could be carried out by hooking onto the links at the shoulders while leaving the hands free to fire weapons if the team was under fire. Weapons are the short XM177E2 SMG version of the M16. (Larry Greene and Society of Vietnamese Rangers)

40. The first major ground unit sent to Vietnam was the 173rd Airborne Brigade pictured here after unloading from choppers on one of their first missions after arriving in 1965. (US Army)

39 ▲ 40 ▼

41. During the 1960s an Air Force PJ is lowered into the sea in full SCUBA gear to carry out a rescue. (USAF)

42. Parachutist's wings locally made in Indo-China and supposedly worn by personnel assigned to Special Operations Group.

43. A. Insignia of Recon Team West Virginia assigned to SOG Command and Control Central out of Kontum. The red Chinese characters to the left of the face stand for 'Kill VC'. The lower Chinese characters stand for 'Lightning Tiger' and 'Recon'.

B. SOG insignia for Command and Control North at Da Nang. The death's head in beret on shell burst was a standard SOG insignia, though it was not normally worn openly. Instead it would be worn sewn inside the beret, etc.

C. Insignia of Command and Control Central. Like the other two SOG insignia this one was locally made in Vietnam. Some SOG insignia will be encountered which were machine-made, but most were hand-made. This insignia and the two preceding are probably both from the late 1960s. Since each Recon Team had their insignia made locally, exact dates cannot be given.

D. Current insignia of Special Forces Operational Detachment A721.

E. Insignia of Special Forces ODA-8, a unit trained for mountain warfare in the Alps.

F. Another current Special Forces insignia, which is illustrative of the fanciful insignia chosen by operational detachment. This one is based on the J. R. R. Tolkien character.

G. 82nd Airborne Division Recondo insignia.

H. Insignia of the 187th Airborne Regimental Combat Team during the Korean War.

I. Insignia worn in Vietnam by the Long-Range Recon Patrols of the 1st Cavalry Division. This same insignia will often be encountered with 'Recon' instead of 'LRRP'.

J. Hand-made insignia worn by members of the 101st Airborne Division's Reconnaissance Unit in Vietnam. 'Sat Cong' means kill Communists; 'Bang Chet' means Shoot to Kill; and 'Ho Kich' means 'Tiger Recon'. Tiger Scouts usually included former VC.

K. Current insignia worn by members of US Navy SEAL Team 2.

L. Current insignia of the USMC 2nd Force Recon Company.

▲41 ▼42

43▶

A

B

C

D

E

F

G

H

I

44. In the mid 1960s, a US Army adviser to the Biet Dong Quan (Vietnamese Rangers) supervises training at the Duc My Ranger Training Center. He wears the MACV (Military Assistance Command Vietnam) shoulder insignia with airborne tab. He also wears the maroon beret of the ARVN Rangers and US

parachutist's wings. The patch on his right pocket denotes the ARVN unit with which he is working. (US Army)

45. Camouflaged trooper of the 82nd Airborne Division offers a good view of the subdued shoulder divisional insignia and arc. (82nd Airborne Division)

▲46 ▼47

46. A US Navy SEAL lies in ambush along a trail in the Mekong Delta. In addition to his old-style, locally-made tiger-stripe utilities, he wears an OD (olive drab) head scarf. Such scarves made from OD towels, bandages, etc., were commonly worn by recon troops in Vietnam because they covered the hair without being as likely to get knocked off in heavy cover as a hat. His weapon is the Stoner M63A1 LMG. The SEALS were very fond of this weapon, though it had a tendency to fire bursts of full automatic fire when dropped. With the 150-round drum as shown, this weapon gave the SEALs a lot of firepower in an ambush. A three-man SEAL ambush party was usually armed with one M63, one Ithaca 12-gauge fighting shotgun, and one M16 with the M203 grenade-launcher affixed. He also carries M26A1 fragmentation grenades. (US Navy)

47. This sergeant is a member of the 9th Infantry Division LRRPs (Long Range Recon Patrol). The black beret as shown was worn by LRRPs in Vietnam for a short time, though it was rarely worn on operations. The beret badge is that of the 9th Infantry DI (Distinctive Insignia). On his jungle utilities he wears the shoulder insignia of the 9th Infantry Division with the LRRP company scroll above it. He also wears an LRRP tab over the badge on his beret. The radio is the URC10 emergency radio widely used by LRRPs and others who operated in enemy territory. (US Army)

48. In Vietnam during the 1960s, an Air Force PJ checks the winch cable on the jungle penetrator aboard a rescue chopper. His maroon beret is tucked into the cargo pocket of his flight suit and he wears a light aircraft crewman's helmet. Barely visible on his name tape are his parachutist's wings and his aircrewman's wings. (USAF)

49. US airborne adviser to the Vietnamese Hac Bao (Black Panther) strike company of the 1st ARVN Infantry Division, and an adviser from the Australian SAS, look over captured weapons. The American, on the right, wears standard green utilities with subdued MACV insignia and airborne tab. His black beret is the beret of the Hac Baos. (Australian War Memorial)

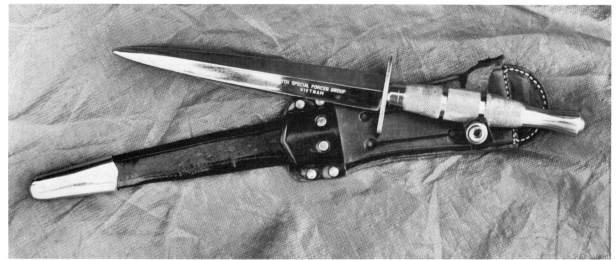

▲50 ▼51

50. Presentation stiletto awarded to some members of the 5th SFG in Vietnam upon completion of their tours of duty.

51. A Special Forces sergeant instructing one of the members of his Mobile Strike Force in correct jumping techniques. On his tiger stripes, this sergeant wears combat infantryman's badge and parachutist's wings in white 'subdued' pattern, and on his left breast the MIKE Force insignia. Note also the 'MIKE FORCE' tape on his left breast. On his green beret he wears what appears to be the old-style 5th SFG flash lacking the yellow with red bands of the Vietnamese flag. As this photograph was taken in 1967, however, after the 5th SFG was well established in Vietnam, it is likely that this is the later flash. (US Army)

52. Insignia worn by the tank destroyer unit of the 101st Airborne Division in Vietnam. A tank is being crushed in the beak of the eagle.

53. General Abrams meets a US Special Forces officer and an ARVN airborne officer at CCN, Danang in 1970. Note that the SF officer (either a major or an LTC) on the right wears both airborne and Ranger tabs over his Special Forces arrowhead insignia on his left shoulder. The beret flash worn by the SF officer is that of the 5th SFG, while the ARVN officer wears the ARVN airborne beret badge on his red beret. (Larry Greene and Society of Vietnamese Rangers)

54. Members of the 173rd Airborne Brigade checking a Vietnamese village for VC. Men of this unit wear the standard full-colour 'Herd' insignia on the left shoulder. Green utilities and helmet with camouflage cover are worn. Weapons are the M16 rifle. (US Army)

52▲

53▼

54▼

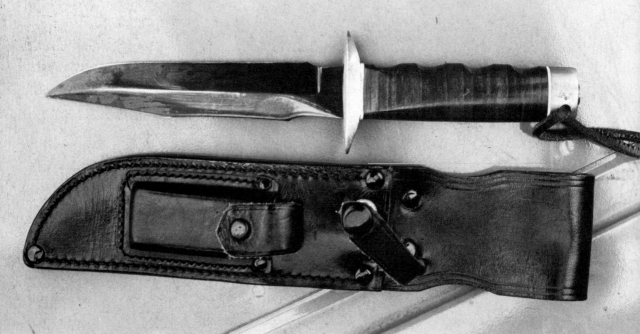

▲56

57▶

55. SEALs going ashore as part of 'Operation Bold Dragon III', March 1968. The SEAL in the centre of the picture wears the camouflage beret sometimes favoured by the SEALs. (US Navy)
56. Bowie-style knife issued to some Special Forces units in Vietnam. This weapon, which is clean of markings, was manufactured on Okinawa and was supposedly issued to SOG units. Not all of these knives, however, are 'clean'; some bear a

small SF beret crest on the blade.
57. Tiger-stripe clad members of the 5th Special Forces Group teach members of a Civilian Irregular Defence Group (CIDG) to use the M79 40mm grenade-launcher. (US Army)

▲58

58. Lightly-equipped USMC Recons return from a patrol, spring 1965. Pistol belt and suspenders as shown were typical of the Marines in the early part of the Vietnam War as were the green fatigues and fatigue hat. (USMC)

59. Two US advisers (middle) to the Vietnamese Rangers are briefed by a Vietnamese officer, mid 1960s. Note that the US captain wears equivalent Vietnamese rank on his shirt front. Both Americans also wear the maroon Ranger beret. (US Army)

60. November 1967. A member of the 173rd Airborne Brigade manning his M60 GPMG looks almost like one of Bill Maulin's Second World War infantrymen. The bottle in the rubber band contains 'bug juice'. The slits in the helmet cover are for the insertion of flora for additional camouflage. OD towels were

frequently worn around the neck to wipe away perspiration. (US Army)

61. A 75th Infantry (Rangers) beret flash locally made in Vietnam. This colourful flash, quartered in blue and olive drab, was derived from the insignia of the 5307th Composite Group (Merrill's Marauders).

62. A US Ranger adviser helps with hand-to-hand combat training of the Vietnamese Rangers, March 1967. In addition to the maroon beret with Viet Ranger beret badge he wears the Ranger insignia on his right pocket. Although such personalized sidearms were frowned on later in the war, he wears a revolver in a commercial US holster. (US Army)

▼59

60 ▲

61 ▲ 62 ▼

63. A soldier of the 82nd Airborne Division uses a flamethrower on a VC hut during an operation in the Republic of Vietnam in 1969. Damp towels under the helmet and over the hands help protect him from the heat. (US Army)

▲ **64** ▼ **65**

66 ▶

64. A soldier of the 173rd Airborne Brigade fires his jeep-mounted 7.62mm M60 at suspected enemy positions during a road security mission, 19–21 February 1969. Note that the machine-gunner wears a flak jacket. The Vietnamese at the lower right wears tiger-striped camouflage utilities. (US Army)

65. US Navy SEALs being debriefed aboard a riverine craft after a mission in Vietnam in September 1967. Note that the two men in the foreground wear the camouflage beret which was the only beret somewhat standardized with the SEALs. (US Navy)

66. Personnel of the 173rd Airborne Brigade firing an 81mm mortar during an operation in Vietnam, May 1965. (US Army)

▲67

67. Members of a SEAL team firing their weapons in the Rung Sat Special Zone in Vietnam, April 1968. The figure fourth from the left has his sling mounted to the top of his M63A1 in the assault position. The SEAL in the right foreground appears to have acquired an AK47. (US Navy)

68. A SEAL places a demolition charge. His flak jacket is in the USMC style with grommets at the bottom for attaching equipment. Tiger-striped boonie hat and utilities are worn. March 1968. (US Navy)

69. SEALs preparing for a mission aboard a riverine patrol craft,

October 1968. The man in the left foreground wears a belt for the Stoner M63 LMG and the man at the right with the headscarf wears a grenadier's vest to carry 40mm grenades. Interestingly, the SEAL at upper right is armed with a Heckler & Koch G3 7.62mm rifle. Distinctive SEAL green camouflage face paint is also visible in this picture. (US Navy)

70. A SEAL, his face camouflaged, and wearing the camouflage beret, waits in ambush along a trail in the Mekong Delta, September 1967. (US Navy)

▼68

▼69

70 ▶

71. A SEAL firing an M60 GPMG from his 'MIKE' boat, September 1967. He wears a flak jacket and over his steel helmet has added his boonie hat. (US Navy)

72. US Navy SEALs moving down the River Bassac on an operation, November 1967. (US Navy)

73. The four-footed SEAL in foreground is 'Silver' with his SEAL handler, summer 1968. 'Silver' was trained to search for enemy bunkers and booby-traps. (US Navy)

▼ 71   72 ▶

▲ 74

▲ 75

74. Left, US parachutist's basic wings; right, US pathfinder wings. The pathfinder is trained to jump in ahead of larger airborne formations and to mark a landing zone for them. Both wings are still in use and have been since the Second World War.
75. Left, the current style of air assault wings; right, the original air assault wings which are now obsolete.
76. LTC Martha Raye visiting men of the 75th Rangers at Fort Hood in 1972. Known world-wide as an entertainer, 'Maggie' Raye holds a particular place in the hearts of the Special Forces and Rangers because of the time she spent touring the boonies in Vietnam. Although her commission is in the Army Nursing Corps, she is fully entitled to the green beret with 5th SFG flash which she is wearing since she is one of only three honorary members of the Special Forces. John Wayne was one of the others. She was presented with a black Ranger beret on this visit. Note that at this time a Ranger arc was worn on the black beret. (US Army)

77. Three USMC Recons show some of the equipment used by this unit. The man in the foreground is equipped for a parachute jump and wears standard Marine Corps helmet and helmet cover. His camouflage utilities were a rarity for Marines until after the Vietnam War and were an indication that a man was serving with a Recon unit. The middle figure is dressed for carrying out the long-range patrols which are the Recons' forte. In addition to his camouflage utilities he wears a boonie hat and carries the famous USMC Ka-Bar fighting/survival knife. The figure on the left is dressed in SCUBA gear and this is indicative of the many beach insertions the Recons make by swimming ashore.
78. A USAF Pararescueman (usually known as a PJ for 'parachute jumper') prepares to descend via a jungle penetrator from a helicopter to rescue a downed aircrewman. Note his distinctive spotted 'leopard' camouflage utilities and his jungle boots. (US Air Force)

▼ 76

▲79 ▼80   ▼81

79. US combat swimmers coming ashore on a beach recon or sabotage exercise. Among the US units containing trained combat swimmers or 'frogmen' are the USMC Recons, US Army Special Forces, US Navy SEALs and UDTs, and USAF CCTs (Combat Control Teams) and Pararescuemen. (Society of Vietnamese Rangers)

80. USAF Combat Controller making a free-fall parachute jump. Note that for free-fall jumps, especially in practice, a crash helmet is normally worn. Standard camouflage utilities are worn beneath the chute, however. (US Air Force)

81. Men of the 82nd Airborne Division, taking part in 'Bright Star' in Egypt, offer a good view of the maroon beret of the 82nd

Airborne and of the desert camouflage pattern used by the 82nd and other US élite forces when serving in the desert. The man on the left holds an M60 GPMG. Beret flashes on the berets of members of the 82nd Airborne normally indicate battalion, but in a few cases such as TOW, engineer, etc., may indicate company.

82. Two USAF CCTs in full SCUBA gear swim ashore to make a beach reconnaissance. CCTs are inserted behind enemy lines – in Vietnam often along the Ho Chi Minh Trail – to call in air strikes or supply other on-site Intelligence for the Air Force. As a result, as with the SEALs and Recons, the CCTs are trained for parachute, small boat, underwater, helicopter, and other types of insertions. (US Air Force)

83. Air Force CCTs training as ski troops for operations in the far north. The white winter ski uniform gives camouflage, while remaining loose enough to allow lightweight but warm clothing to be worn beneath it. (US Air Force)

84. Men of the 1st Battalion, 75th Infantry (Ranger) standing to attention at Fort Stewart, Georgia, 1980s. These Rangers wear the black Ranger beret, and the Ranger scroll on the left shoulder. Their utilities are woodland-pattern. (US Army)

85. On an exercise in the 1980s, troops of the 1st Battalion, 75th

Rangers apply face camouflage to one another at Fort Lewis, WA. (US Army)

86. Men of the 75th Rangers in Regenburg, a mock city built at Fort Lewis for training in urban warfare. (US Army)

87. A corporal currently serving with the 75th Rangers puts the finishing touches to his face camouflage. Subdued rank insignia are worn on the collar and a Ranger arc is worn on his utility cap. A steel helmet, however, is also available on his pistol belt. (US Army)

◀ 83

84 ▼

85 ▼

86 ▼

87 ▼

▲88 ▼89

88. Rangers in cold-weather training at Fort Richardson, Alaska, in the 1980s, pulling an Akio. (US Army)

89. A member of the 75th Rangers, just after completing a jump. (US Army)

90. A Ranger stringing barbed wire offers a good view of the leaf- or woodland-pattern camouflage jacket. (US Army)

91. After jumping from a C-123, a trooper of the 75th Rangers prepares to collapse his chute and remove it. (US Army)

90▲ 91▼

▲92

▲93

92. A determined looking Ranger prepares to board an aircraft for a night jump. Ranger arc and Airborne Ranger scroll are visible on his left shoulder. (US Army)

93. Insignia worn by Special Forces aviation personnel, both chopper pilots and aircrewmen.

94. With more than 100lb of equipment strapped on, these present-day 75th Rangers wait to emplane aboard the C-123 in the background. Short haircuts are very typical of the Rangers who are very proud of their élite status and are not in the least worried about blending into the civilian population when off duty. (US Army)

95. Members of the US Army Special Forces give small boat training during a survival course for men of the 3rd Infantry Division at Bad Tolz, Germany. (US Army)

96. Two Navy SEALs board a Sea Knight helicopter at Subic Bay in the Philippines in preparation for a jump, August 1978. (US Navy)

94 ▲

95 ▲ 96 ▼

97. A SEAL team officer briefs his men prior to a training exercise in April 1974. His utilities are leaf-pattern camouflage and his much worn boonie hat may well be a veteran of the Vietnam War. (US Navy)

98. Gerber fighting/survival knife used by men of the 1st SFG.

99. Men of the 7th SFG wearing full packs and their green berets, demonstrate rappelling techniques. Late 1970s or early 1980s. (US Army)

◀ **97**

98 ▲ **99** ▼

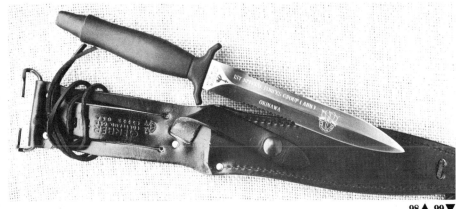

▲100 ▼101

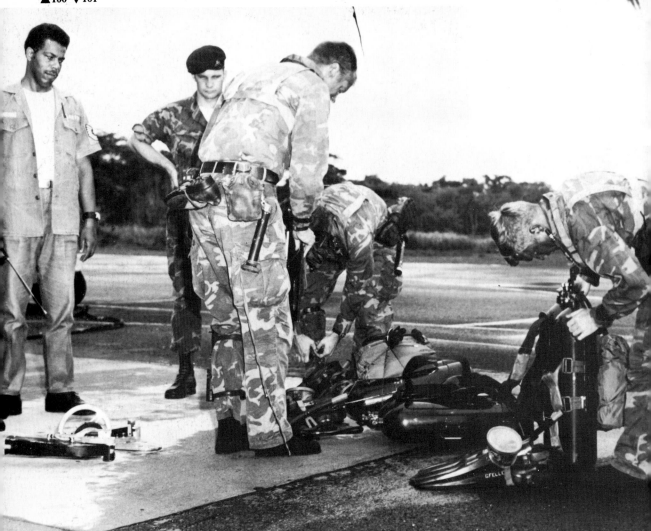

100. Left is the beret badge of the USAF Combat Control Teams; right, the beret badge of the USAF Pararescuemen. The CCT beret badge is a relatively recent adoption, US parachutist's wings having been worn as a beret badge by this unit during the Vietnam War.

101. During the late 1970s or early 1980s, members of a USAF Combat Control Team prepare their equipment for a 'wet jump' into the sea. The man second from left wears the dark blue beret of the CCTs. (US Air Force)

102. Members of an Air Force Combat Control Team leave a helicopter via a trooper ladder. Men are armed with M16s and S & W Model 15 revolvers. (US Air Force)

103. Air Force PJs making a parachute jump, during the late 1960s or early 1970s. (US Air Force)

◀102

▲104 ▼105

104. July 1972. A captain assigned to the 7th SFG underwater detachment in Panama explains the necessity for removing reefs to make the passage of large craft to Pedro Jacinto Cevallo safer. The man second from the right wears what appears to be an SF SCUBA Detachment insignia on his shorts. The captain on the right wears the red flash of the 7th SFG beneath his captain's bars. Enlisted personnel wear the SF crest on the flash, while officers wear their rank insignia. Subdued SF insignia and airborne arc are worn on the captain's left shoulder. The major, on the left, wears a 2nd Infantry Division insignia on his right shoulder indicating combat experience with that unit, probably in the Korean War since the 2nd Infantry Division did not serve in Vietnam. (US Army)

105. In June 1971, officers of the 8th SFG discuss the progress of a counter-insurgency exercise in Panama. (US Army)

106. A member of the Special Forces, attending the USMC sniper school in 1981, wears part of a camouflage 'ghillie' suit and carries a heavy-barrelled sniper's rifle. (US Army)

106 ▶

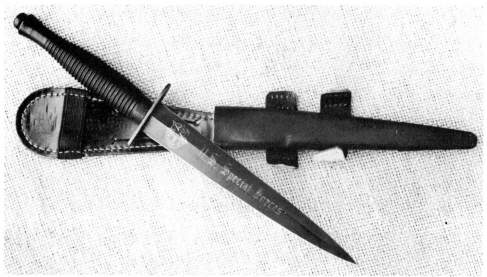

▲108

▲109 ▼110

107. (Previous spread) Members of the 7th SFG moving down a stream show good counter ambush technique as they look to opposite sides. Leaf-pattern camouflage is worn and the M56 webbed gear in fighting load mode is worn. As is often the case with SF, a diversity of weapons can be seen. The lead man carries an Uzi 9mm SMG, the second man an M16, and the third man an AK47. (Society of Vietnamese Rangers)

108. F-S stiletto carried by members of the 10th SFG in Europe.

109. Ka-Bar fighting/survival knife used by members of ODA-732 (Operational Detachment A-732) of the 7th SFG.

110. Diver's knife used by members of the Special Forces Europe SCUBA Detachment.

111. A member of the 11th SFG and an instructor from the SEALs discuss foreign weapons, 1981. All the weapons are of East European origin apart from a French MAT-49 SMG (second on the right, foreground). (US Army)

112. Two members of the Society of Vietnamese Rangers who are also Congressional Medal of Honor winners pose together. Colonel Lewis Millett, on the left, won his Medal of Honor for a bayonet charge during the Korean War. On the right is FSG Gary Littrell. Both men wear Vietnamese Ranger badges on the right breast. Colonel Millett also wears Vietnam parachutist's wings on his right breast. Note that in addition to master parachutist's wings, Sergeant Littrell also wears air assault wings. (Society of Vietnamese Rangers)

111▲ 112▼

▲113 ▼114

113. During the 'Bright Star' manoeuvres, members of the 82nd Airborne prepare to jump in Egypt with Egyptian paratroopers. The captain on the left confers with his Egyptian opposite number before emplaning. Note that although the Egyptian officer still wears his red beret, he carries the Egyptian jump helmet in his left hand. (See para at left of photo for this helmet in wear.) The US paratroopers wear the desert camo pattern. (82nd Airborne)

114. Men of the 82nd Airborne Division during recent 'Bright Star' exercises in Egypt, wearing the desert camouflage pattern.

Note also the goggles to keep sand out of the eyes while driving in the desert. (82nd Airborne Division)

115. Two members of the 82nd Airborne Division check each other's packs before a forced march. As the Army's most combat-ready division, the 82nd Airborne is often called upon to test new equipment. These troopers, for example, wear the Army's new helmet which will replace the venerable M1. They also wear the camouflage BDU (Battle Dress Uniform). (82nd Airborne Division)

115▼

116. Radio man of the 82nd Airborne Division with his equipment during a recent exercise. Note that the new experimental Army helmet is worn by both men and that a blank firing device is fitted to the M-16 rifle of the man in the background. (82nd Airborne Division)

117. Members of the 82nd Airborne Division prepare to fire the TOW (Tube-launched Optically-tracked, Wire-guided) anti-tank missile during recent exercises. (82nd Airborne Division)

118. Heavy weapons leaders of the 7th SFG teach artillery tactics to Guatemalan troops in the autumn of 1973. Members of this SF detachment wear typical 'Gaut' utilities so as to be less obtrusive. The tattoo on the arm of the man in the left foreground is of a typical dancing girl whose hips will sway when the forearm muscles are 'rolled'. (US Army)

◄116

117▲ 118▼

119. A member of the 11th SFG prepares to make a parachute jump, while the jumpmaster checks his equipment. (US Army)
120. A member of the 75th Ranger gains control of his chute while struggling to maintain his balance, despite the equipment container strapped to his left leg. This photograph was taken on an exercise during the last few years. (US Army)

◀119 ▼120

▲122   ▼123

121. (Previous spread) Members of the 75th Rangers take part in an exercise in Regenburg, a mock city constructed at Fort Lewis, WA. March 1980. (US Army photo)

122. At Bad Tolz, Germany, HQ for the Special Forces Detachment assigned to Europe, men from the 3rd Infantry Division learn survival procedures from men of the Special Forces during the winter of 1973. (US Army)

123. During a recent exercise a member of the 75th Rangers applies face camouflage to one of his buddies. (US Army)